Creative Literacy: English GCSE

Amanda J Harrington

author of the Creative Writing for Kids series

and Creative Writing for Adult Learners

Copyright © Amanda J. Harrington 2013.

Creative Writing for Adult Learners © Amanda J Harrington 2013

Front cover created using an original image by © Mega11 | Dreamstime.com

The right of Amanda J. Harrington to be identified as author

of this work has been asserted by her in accordance with

the Copyright, Designs and Patents Act 1988.

All rights reserved. No part of this book may be reproduced,

transmitted or stored in an information retrieval system in

any form or by any means, graphic, electronic or mechanical,

including photocopying, taping and recording,

without prior written permission from the publisher

978-1-291-43258-9

Contents

Introduction.. 7

How to use this book.. 8

Section 1: the rain comes 11

One.. 12

Two 17

Three 21

Four.. 26

Five 29

Six 32

Seven.. 35

Eight... 39

Nine.. 41

Ten 46

Eleven 49

Twelve 56

Thirteen 59

Fourteen 62

Fifteen 68

Sixteen 73

Seventeen 76

Section 2: Original Writing & Language 79

Creative Renovation 80

The Knitting Witch 81

Sammy Saves the Day 86

The Dreaded Letter Writing 89

Diary of a dog-walker 92

Join the club! 94

Then and now 98

Story Starters.. 102

In the movies... 106

Genre.. 107

The Plot.. 110

A scene... 112

Characters 114

Action Scene 116

The Twist 118

Where? 119

Why me? 120

Almost there... 122

The winner! 124

Page | 6

Introduction

GCSE students and those coming up to their GCSE study years will find this book a valuable resource in learning how to answer complex exam and coursework questions. At the same time, students who need more practice and improvement will develop new skills and techniques.

All the work in this book has been used by GCSE and pre-GCSE students, for independent study as well as in lessons. It can be adapted to suit different abilities or to help with specific work.

This book is split into **three main sections**.

Comprehension & literary criticism: Comprehension, literary criticism and language exploration based around one fiction book, 'the rain comes' by Amanda J Harrington.

'the rain comes' is available to buy on Amazon, but may be studied through this book without needing the complete text.

Original writing & language work: General language exercises, designed to help the student practice and develop their original writing and English language skills, including grammar and punctuation, as well as writing style.

In-depth writing: A longer-length, complete original writing activity which develops different writing skills and helps students think more deeply about how they write and why.

How to use this book

Comprehension & literary criticism: Extracts from 'the rain comes' are used as a basis for literacy work, with the emphasis on drawing out the student's understanding of the text and helping them to express themselves. All questions have clear **guidelines** on how to answer, as well as **suggestions** on what to include, so that less confident students are not just faced with the questions.

The questions and exercises explore the use of language in the extracts, the hidden meanings and implied thoughts and feelings of the characters. There is detailed analysis of how the characters behave and why. Students are constantly challenged to delve deeper into the text and explain their own answers.

The extracts are easy to read, while offering deeper, complex and sensitive themes, such as grief, loss, love, abandonment, trust, faith and freedom. 'the rain comes' is accessible to most students and the work in this book can be completed flexibly, to suit different abilities.

There are also creative writing exercises within the book, based around 'the rain comes' but with freedom to create new scenarios and re-write situations for the characters. This supports students who need to improve their original writing, while giving them confidence by basing the writing on texts they have studied throughout the book.

Original writing & language work: This section has a wide variety of work, covering work which mirrors what is given in exams and coursework, as well as introducing students to new methods of creative writing.

Guidelines are given throughout this section, with suggestions on what can be included in answers. There are also explanations as to what should be included when answering these types of questions in exams so that students know what is expected of them.

The work in this section can be done at any time, but forms a good foundation for study before attempting the third section of the book.

In-depth writing: This section has more challenging and developed writing ideas, which test the student's ability to create different work for a variety of scenarios. Throughout this section, they must put themselves into the minds of their characters and create ideas which are expanded as they progress through the work.

To help with this more challenging section, I have included lots of example answers so that students are not alone when doing their own work. They have the chance to see how I have answered the question, so they know how they can approach it themselves.

Section 1: the rain comes

The first section of this book uses one source, '**the rain comes**', to help develop English Language and Literature skills. By using one source material, you gain confidence in talking about different areas of literacy, which helps you to achieve more with the standard texts and exercises given in school.

'the rain comes' is a short book with an unusual structure. The first section tells us Maria's story and is written in a semi-disjointed style, as Maria grows to understand where she is and what has happened to her.

The middle section takes us back through time, alongside the people who feature strongly in Maria's life, giving the reader insights into Maria and her story, as well as showing us what happens to her loved ones after her death.

The final section is from the point of view of Maria's great-nephew, James. This is written in a normal style, with the structure mirroring the start of the book, as James uncovers Maria's mystery without realising the role he plays.

One

Look at the following extract from 'the rain comes'. This is the first chapter and is also the beginning of Maria's story. Read it through then answer the questions.

***

I can hear wind. Strange, how everything else fades away, leaving me with the sound of trees soughing outside. So, I suppose I can hear the trees really, when I think of it. I don't often think of it, though. Sometimes the wind has been blowing for a long time before I turn my face towards it, turn my face away from the door.

Turning my face towards a window? I don't know that either. We always expect sounds to come more clearly through a window. I can't see a window, or the walls, I only see the door. Sometimes, if I try very hard, I can hold up my hands and see glimpses of them, as if I blink, very slowly, the darkness creeping over me. It's like I fall asleep when I blink, only needing that momentary darkness to slip away. No dreams though. Never those.

When I hear the wind, the trees, I think of rain and storms

lashing against the house at night. Then I fall away again. But for that moment, I can feel the way it used to feel to be here, in the house, alone, the weather beating its way in and me, laying in my bed, waiting to see if tonight, it would come to me.

When Jessie used to knock on the door, afraid, I'd let her in and gently chide her for being silly. I'd never been afraid of the storms, just wary. You have to respect the elements, I would say. God gave the earth to us, but we are small creatures still.

That was a long thought for me. I haven't remembered Jessie in a long time. I wonder, if I could see my hands, would they have tears on them? Would they be my tears?

Yesterday, I'll call it that, I heard something else and then blinked myself to sleep. I haven't been awake enough to hear anything. Like the thoughts of Jessie, it was something new. I tried to turn my head, found I could not. I tried - I don't know what I tried, I was gone soon enough.

Today, I still can't see my hands. Why is it important? I can feel them. I feel them there, at the ends of my arms, I think. I can't make them touch, though, so perhaps they are in my imagination? Perhaps I don't even blink.

I heard the wind today, but no rain. I want to think of the rain. And Jessie. I want to be able to-

I heard the wind and it wasn't the trees. Like a moment of waking, I heard the wind blow in through a door! If I could move, I cannot move.

Was it today that I heard the door? Is it raining yet? If I was able to snuggle down in my bed, would it be night and the storm? Would Jessie come and it would all be as it was?

Can I see my hands? Are they my tears?

I can hear the -

I turn my head. I see no window, but I hear the window. I hear the rain hitting the glass. I have a window. I can hear the rain.

I hear the door.

***

1. What are your first impressions of Maria?

Write a few sentences explaining how you feel about her as a character and what kind of person you think she is. Include at least 2 quotes from the extract. Don't be afraid to give an opinion.

2. What are your first impressions of the style and structure of the book?

Look at the extract again. How are the sentences arranged? How do some of them end? Are they all complete? Do they leave you without answers?

This can be a difficult question to answer, so if you are struggling, come back to this question once you have worked on more of the book.

3. Describe the type of language used in this extract.

You should look for the descriptive words used. Do they follow a pattern? Do they repeat? If they do repeat or follow a pattern, what does this mean for the reader? Choose a few good examples, either single words or phrases, to show the type of language used.

4. Why do you think Jessie may be important in the book?

This is a question where you need to give an opinion which

you support with evidence from the text. For instance, you can say Jessie is important because she is mentioned in the very first chapter (this is not enough of an answer, so don't just copy!).

5. What do you think is going to happen next?

Write a few sentences for this one. It doesn't matter if you are totally wrong, the aim of a story is to make you think and part of the fun can be in getting it wrong and being surprised as you read on.

Explaining what you think or expect is a good way to practice thinking about language and literature in general. You become used to looking at extracts and full works as something you can deal with in stages. You don't have to know everything at once to be able to work things out and answer questions.

Two

This extract is another part of Maria's story. This time we learn more about her past. It is still disjointed, but reads more like a normal story. Read through, taking particular notice of the language and what you are told about other characters.

***

When I was three, I found a frog in the garden. Father let me keep it for a little while. Mother was out for the day.

The garden used to be my playroom, so warm in the sun.

In the wind, I hid under the trees, watching the branches swaying above me. I loved the way the leaves jittered and danced. I loved the wind.

Father let me keep the frog for a little while. I think Mother was out.

I sat in the garden, waiting for Jessie.

I sat in the garden, watching her pram. She had to have fresh air.

I rocked her pram but she woke and I was spanked.

I told her stories. Does she remember them? Does Jessie remember me?

Jessie was in her pram, in the garden.

I found a frog, I think I remembered that already.

When I was five, Jessie was born. I rocked her pram.

Mother brought the glasses out into the garden and we had tea in the sunshine.

The kitchen was new, it was green. I wanted yellow.

Jessie was in her pram and we had tea in the garden. I rocked her pram. I think that was another time.

When Mother had tea in the garden, I was afraid. Mother hated the garden.

Father wasn't coming home. He wouldn't have any tea.

We had tea. I was afraid.

***

1. Separate and list the information given in this extract.

For instance, how does Maria remember things? What does she think of her mother?

Even if you don't understand all of the information given, try to split it up into groups. So you might have more information on the frog and Maria's father, but you could also say something about how Maria feels as a separate group.

2. What information do we have about Maria's mother and father in this extract?

Find words or phrases which give you information about these characters. For instance, Maria's father lets her keep the frog. What does this suggest about him as a person?

3. Write some sentences about the confused nature of time in this extract.

Read the extract again and work out the order of events. Maria gets mixed up in her memories and also forgets she has already remembered things.

4. If everything was described in the right order, how would it change the way it feels to read this extract?

You need more descriptive sentences here, as well as your own opinions. How would it feel to read a standard description of these events? Would they make more sense? Would they seem as dream-like? How would it change what we know about Maria and her confusion?

5. What does this extract add to the whole story?

You don't need to read the whole story to comment on this. In the first section, Maria tries to work out where she is and what has happened. In this section, she is looking into the past and doesn't mention the present at all.

Think about what it adds to a story to talk about the past. What do you find out about the characters?

Three

This next extract deals with Edgar. He is an important character throughout the book and this is where we first meet him.

Read through the extract and take notice of Maria's confusion and the way it helps us understand how she feels.

You might want to consider how we are supposed to respond to Edgar. This is a good passage to come back to when you have studied more of the book and know Edgar, and the other characters, a little better.

***

When I was asleep, I always had dreams. It was like an escape.

Now my whole life is a dream. It was dream-like before, lying in my bed.

Now, when I blink, sometimes it's still dark. Other times, I see faded images of the past, I'm there again. I don't know I'm dreaming till I find myself here.

I long to see the garden. I long for so much. Mother said Father had died.

Edgar read to me. Mother liked him so he came every third day and read to me. Mother said she didn't want me to be stupid.

Edgar told me I wasn't stupid. He smiled. Mother liked him so I was worried. I wondered if Father would have liked him?

When I was eighteen, Edgar read to me. Mother liked him and I was still worried. He started reading poetry. I don't like most of it, some of it sounds like the wind.

He started by reading me poetry. He never asked what I wanted to hear.

Mother gave him a book of poetry to read to me. He left it open on the bed, I saw her name in it.

Mother liked Edgar so I was worried. He read me old books, long, boring books. He had a nice voice.

When I was eighteen, Edgar read to me. He read the long, old book.

He read the old book, then he paused and he looked -

He paused and he read the old book -

The words were new.

The words were from the newspaper.

My father had married again. My father was alive.

Edgar paused and read from the long, old book.

He held the book with one hand, he put the other across my wrist and -

Edgar read quietly, I heard none of it.

When he had finished, I turned my face to him and he wiped away my tears.

'I'm glad he isn't dead,' I whispered.

'I know,' he said.

***

1. Look at the extract and separate it into main sections. Describe how Edgar is introduced, how Maria's mother is involved and how Maria feels. Also include the extra information about Maria's father.

By splitting texts up in this way, even if you only do it mentally, without writing it down, you are helping yourself to look at them critically. You begin to see them as creative works which have been put together in a certain order for a reason. This then helps you to write about them and gain more understanding of them.

2. What are we meant to think of Edgar after reading this?

Look at the information we are given. How is Edgar presented? Separate what he does from Maria's doubt towards him.

3. What extra information does this extract give us about Maria's mother?

Maria's mother isn't mentioned in much detail but what is said is important. What does Maria's doubt over her mother liking Edgar tell us?

This is where you need to make decisions based not just on what a text tells you but also on what is left out. For instance, in this extract we find out very little about Edgar but he does something very important: what does this *imply* about his role in the story?

4. What feelings are implied between Maria and Edgar?

Again, you need to give an opinion here. Base it on what happens in the text and also include quote/s to support what you say.

Four

This next extract gives us more solid information about Maria's past, as well as suggestions about her future.

***

Edgar came to see me and Mother wouldn't let him come up. She raised her voice, he didn't raise his. Jessie cried.

That night, Jessie let him in to see me. He said goodbye.

Jessie held me as I cried.

I barely cry.

Edgar never really talked to me, he read to me, poetry and old books. They weren't even love poems or love stories.

His voice was gentle, he paused and looked across at me and smiled.

I was worried because Mother liked him. Jessie told me his father was rich. Mother and Edgar's father used to know each other. Mother had told them I would get well.

I remember Jessie telling me this as she held me and I cried. I cried more then. Had Edgar known, when he met me, that I wouldn't get well? Had he known and read to me anyway?

Did he look at me and believe me when I tried to look better and happy?

I don't think Edgar believed anything like that.

He paused and smiled, he gently held my wrist and he knew I wouldn't get better.

Edgar told me goodbye and he held me in his arms. He kissed my hair and said, if he could, he would carry me away and keep me safe.

We both knew I wouldn't be safe.

***

1. Think about the other extracts you have read and explain how this one moves the story forward.

This is quite a difficult question so don't be worried if you take more time to answer. Think about what you know so far. Note the main facts you have, about Maria and the other people in her life.

Now, look again at this extract. How much more information does it give? For instance, the relationships between Maria and Edgar, as well as Maria and other people.

2. Why is this extract more dramatic than the others?

Think about how you feel when you read it. Is Maria in danger? Will she see Edgar again? Can Jessie keep her safe? What will the mother do?

Try to support your answer with evidence from the extract, but if necessary, bring in evidence from earlier extracts. You can also make statements based on how you feel after reading this and the other extracts. For instance, you might want to say that you feel fear for Maria when you read it because of how afraid she is of her mother.

3. What does this extract tell us about the characters of Edgar and Jessie?

There isn't lots of information about them but use evidence from the texts to support how you think they are portrayed as characters.

4. What do you think might happen next?

Five

Now we move to the next part of Maria's story. We don't find out the truth about her until later in the book, but this extract hints at what happened, while showing her confusion over the past.

***

I always liked the candles on my cake. It was so hot, when it burned. Too many candles at twenty four. Was Jessie coming to my party?

I wondered if she would come in her wedding dress? Mother wouldn't let her in.

I wanted to see if she had a husband. You needed a husband if you were married.

The candles were hot on the cake.. Would it be melted? Would it still taste like cake?

I remember hearing the flapping of the kitchen door -

Flapping of the kitchen door, but she didn't come up. There was no tray.

I really must have a fever.

I couldn't move, I was too weak.

Is the bed made? She asked this a lot, is the bed made? Who makes the bed, Mother makes it. Is the bed made?

Every time lately, a real habit.

If I wasn't so weak, I think I would go mad.

Is the bed made? Yes, it's made. I can't move, the bedclothes are too tight.

When Jessie comes, she might be wearing -

The bed was made, I couldn't get up.

I didn't have a fever.

Too many candles? Did I have a cake?

I didn't have a fever, I don't have a fever? Why am I so hot?

***

1. What are your first impressions of this extract?

Make this quite a long answer. Include what you actually think and feel about it, as well as mentioning the language used.

2. Explain what the confused time structure brings to this extract.

Think of the use of tense: past, present and future. How does this help us to understand Maria? Can we work out some of what happened because of the structure? For instance, if it was written in the right order, then Maria wouldn't mention Jessie's wedding dress.

3. What do you think Maria's state of mind is at this point?

Use evidence from the text to support your answer. Don't forget to include how she is feeling and how her confused thoughts affect her emotions.

4. Describe how Maria's mother is portrayed in this extract.

Are we getting a clearer picture of her mother? How does she make Maria feel?

Six

Now we move towards the present and Maria's realization of what has happened to her. Read the following extract, thinking of the ones that have gone before.

***

It's so dark and I'm afraid. Then I realise it's only night and I feel the fear fall away. It's like breathing after holding my breath too long. Is the moon out?

I turn to the window. Now the whole room is dark. Before, I imagined the room. Now I feel the room around me. How long was it away? How long was I gone? Where did I go?

I see it's night-time so I want to get up and go to the window. Mother never let me get up at night. I was always tucked in, tight as can be.

When I was older, I felt like she listened. I didn't dare get up.

Mother has gone, she isn't here anymore. Will I see Jessie if I get up? No, it's night and it's been a long time. Has it been as long as one of Edgar's books?

Page | 32

I want to see the moon and as I think it, I do it. I feel my legs swing away from the bed. I almost feel he bed. I feel the floor. My feet are bare.

I don't stagger. It must be earlier than when I was twenty four. I know this doesn't make sense, I must be older than twenty four. Did I get better and forget? Is Mother dead?

I reach the window and feel its cold glass against my hands. There is no glass. I feel it still. I see there is no glass.

I look out and see the streetlights. I can't see the moon. I need to go out to the garden. Can I get that far?

If there is no glass, will there be no door? Will there be no garden? Will the trees be there?

I turn towards the door.

***

1. How is the tone of this extract different from the others?

This is a big question. Compare the way this one feels, the language used, the emotions in it, to the ones based in her past. Does she still feel fear? Is she still in danger?

Don't forget to mention any important language or use quotes to support what you say.

2. What new information are we given in this extract?

Include information about Maria and other people. What do we now know or suspect, that we didn't before? For instance, her mother has gone, though we don't know how or why yet.

3. This extract talks more about the house and surroundings than the others. How does this add to the story?

Think about how Maria feels about her home. Include what she wants to do or what she used to enjoy.

Also, think of how the description of the house seems to change between past and present. What does this tell us about Maria and her situation? Are things as they used to be?

Seven

We are almost at the end of Maria's story. This extract shows her understanding growing. Take particular notice of the language and structure as you read it.

***

The door is black because it was burned but, unlike the glass, the door is still there.

I feel so sad when I realise I didn't need to open the door. I knew really, when I could think. But too many unshed tears, I didn't want more.

I'm in the hallway. I didn't need to open the door but I can feel the soft carpet under my feet. Everything has changed.

Lovely, gentle colours everywhere. The front door has lots of glass in it, the sunset is falling through in soft waves across the downstairs hall.

This isn't my home anymore. I'm not afraid. Mother has gone.

The kitchen door has gone. There's just an empty space. The

cupboards have gone too, it's all empty with pipes sticking out. The back door is open.

I look to the right, towards the parlour. The door is open. I don't want to go, but I do. I need to see, to make sure she's gone.

The room is not hers anymore. There is colour everywhere, toys all over the floor, painted pictures on the walls, a blanket over an old armchair. The window looks out to a wide, sweeping drive where the front garden used to be.

I'm suddenly worried. Is the garden still there? My trees. I turn back towards the kitchen. I must pass through it to get out to the back garden.

I move across the hall, the beautiful tiled floor cool under my feet. I can look down now. My nightdress, the one I hated. It still had plenty of wear in it.

The kitchen floor is colder, no covering at all. There is a breeze through the back door. I reach out towards it and hear voices behind me.

I don't turn at first, I clasp my hands to my chest. I can see them now, they are hands, I do have them still. There are no tears on them.

I have to be brave. Now that Mother is gone, there is no fear anymore. I turn -

***

1. How is the structure of this extract different from the others?

Think about the length and type of sentences used. Is this one easier to follow? Is it all in the proper order?

2. Explain how Maria feels in this extract.

Focus on language for this question and use quotes from the text to support your answer. How does the choice of words reflect Maria's new emotions?

3. Think of the colours and images used in this extract. How do they affect the overall impression?

Lots of colours are used in this extract, as well as images which have not appeared before in the story. How do they change how we, and Maria, feel about the house and what has happened around her? What kind of emotions do they suggest to the reader? What kind of house has it become?

Don't be afraid to compare the house as it appears now with how it was presented in earlier extracts. This is a good way to support any statements you make, especially when talking about how Maria feels.

4. How aware is Maria now?

Explain how much she understands of her situation now and of the changes around her. Is she now completely aware, or is she still a little confused?

Eight

Look at the following extract and write about how it makes you feel as a reader.

Concentrate on the words used, the way it affects you after what has been described in the other extracts and what it suggests about a possible ending to Maria's story.

How do you think Maria feels at this point? Do her feelings affect the way you, as a reader, respond to this extract?

***

I blinked again. It's almost light. The sun is rising up behind the house, a cool light coming across the kitchen. It has furniture in it now. They don't look like the old ones. A woman is singing as she waits for the kettle to boil.

She lets a tea-spoon fall from her hand and the song stops in mid-note. She pauses a moment, then, without turning, looks to one side.

'If I turn around, will you be there?' she whispers. 'Please, be there, Maria.'

I cover my hands with my mouth, afraid to speak. She turns, very, very slowly. I'm almost too afraid to wait, but Mother is gone and there is no fear.

Jessie came back for me.

Nine

This extract is from the next section of the book and is from Jessie's point of view.

***

I'm meant to be at the doctor's today. I hurt my hand at school and they said I should get it checked out. I was clever, for once, pretending I'd got pain so that Mother would let me come into town. So, just for this little while, I've come into a café and I'm going to sit here and be one of the crowd. A normal person, on her way to or from somewhere. Maybe I'm meeting my sister for lunch or –

God, no, I don't want to cry in public. What a life that would be, if I could meet Maria for lunch or go shopping or anything. Instead, I have to go home, from my little oasis here, and see her bedroom door closed, with Mother guarding access at all times. Stupid, stupid woman! I hate her so much!

'I'm all right, thank you,' I can't even answer properly, why do people have to be kind as well as normal? Can't they see I need to be left alone? Can't they tell I'm not really here? I feel like they should be able to see through me.

I'd better go soon, I need time to make my face look right, to hide the tears. It was a nice rest, I'll have to see if I can re-visit it in bed tonight. Just one more look round the café, burn it all into my mind's eye for later, the colours, smells, sounds, the –

He's seen me! What do I do? I must look different now, he won't know it's me, not after all this time. I was only a – oh no, he's getting up. I have to go!

I try to run out of the café and nearly bump into an old man coming in. He grasps me by the arm as I tumble sideways.

'Careful!' he says, his eyes creasing at the corners. 'You don't have to rush everywhere, there's plenty of time,'

There isn't, though. Edgar has caught up with me. The old man passes by and I'm forced to turn and smile and try not to blush any more, though that would be amazingly impossible as I'm blushing enough for at least every woman in the place. Though if they had Edgar looking down at them, with that smile on his face, they would probably blush too.

Oh, for heaven's sake, I'm like a child! I'll just make my excuses and leave, he can see I'm busy, he knows I won't be able to stay. Doesn't he?

'You can't be cantering about like that,' he says, his voice quiet like I remember. Well, a minor miracle, it turns out I have some extra blush left in me.

'Um,' I manage. Um? What on earth is um?

'Do you have to go?' he asks, 'Maybe we could have another coffee?'

'I don't drink coffee,' I hear myself whisper. If I had a third leg, I'd use it to kick myself.

'Can you stay for a minute?' he asks, putting a hand out to the table I just left.

I look to the corner, where he was sitting. There's a man there, maybe his father? He seems to be reading something. I don't think he's taking any notice. He's turned a bit away from us, so maybe he isn't even interested. Maybe I could stay, just a tiny, little, miniscule time?

I look at my watch. 'I have seven minutes before my bus leaves,' I say.

'When do you have to be home?' he asks, his smile turning to concern.

'In half an hour - on the dot,' I add.

'We'll give you a lift, then you can stay longer.' I glance at the man again but he's still reading. 'Will your mother be waiting at the bus stop?' Edgar asks.

'No, she won't leave the house,' I say, starting to feel excited. Is this how normal people feel too? Like happy, but with added fizz?

'Good,' Edgar says, sitting down quickly and pulling out the chair next to him. He turns his smile on me, not the kind one I'm used to, another, an unfamiliar one. I realise I'm staring at him, at this bright face of his I never saw before. I always liked Edgar but, where did this face come from? It's like light shines out of him. Were his eyes always this blue?

I touch my cheek and realise I'm smiling back.

***

1. Using evidence from the text, describe Jessie's personality.

How does she appear? What words are used by her?

2. How is Edgar portrayed in this extract?

Think about how he is described physically, as well as how he makes Jessie feel. What does he do and say to add to your impression of his personality?

3. What are Jessie's feelings and attitudes towards her mother?

Support with evidence from the text, as well as any implied information, such as Jessie being brave enough to lie so she can escape for a while.

4. How significant is it that Jessie is portrayed in the surroundings of the coffee shop, compared to Maria in the house?

This is an open-ended question, where you can write about how Jessie's surroundings are the opposite of Maria's. You can also mention their different personalities, how Jessie is allowed out into the world and is a part of it.

Is the coffee shop the shape of things to come for Jessie, compared to Maria? Is she destined to live a life surrounded by people rather than being trapped at home?

Ten

This extract is from Edgar's first full section in the book. As you read it, think of how he has been portrayed up to now, through the eyes of other people.

***

I feel like I've been crying forever and it's only been minutes, seconds really. Holding little Samantha, standing, helpless. All I can do is hold the baby. All I can do is stand here and wonder if we'll still be a family by morning. Can't they turn off that beeping? How can they work with it going on and on around them? It's driving me insane!

All I can do is be here, how am I supposed to do anything? Little Samantha isn't even crying, she just makes snuffling noises. It's like she's waiting to see what happens. Does she feel the same as I do? Do babies have full hearts, when they're born? Will she remember this terrible night?

It's not a terrible night, I can't call it that. Our little girl was born and this will be her birthday, year after year. I want that woman in there to be at every party, making every cake, seeing her little girl blowing out the candles. It can't be this way! She has to see Sam blow out her candles! I can't do it, not without her.

I know I can, if I have to. Oh Lord, don't make me have to do it alone, don't let it be like it was for Dad. Don't make me have to create a mother for Samantha out of memories and dreams I have in my empty bed? I can only do this the once, this love, this husband and wife. I wasn't made for anyone else, Lord.

No, I can't ask just for me. I've known Jessie, we've had time. Not enough, but it would never be enough. For Samantha, Lord, just for her. Please.

***

1. How is Edgar's personality developed in this extract?

The key word in this question is 'developed'. We have already seen a lot of Edgar in the book and have built up an impression of him. Now we read his own words, honest words which describe a difficult time in his life.

What more do we learn about him here? Do we have past impressions confirmed by how he is in this extract? Is there anything different about him, that you didn't expect?

2. Describe the relationship between Edgar and Jessie.

What does this extract tell us about them? You can include information from the coffee shop scene too.

3. How does this extract link to Maria's story?

This is a hard one! You need to think about Maria's story as a whole, the main elements of her struggle and suffering, as well as the important roles played by Jessie and Edgar.

How would the birth of baby Samantha and the threat to Jessie's life link to this earlier struggle? Is there anything similar? Can you link their suffering? What about the love shown between Edgar and Jessie, as well as the love of Edgar for his new daughter? Can you link this, even to compare, with Maria and the relationships she had with other people?

Eleven

Before reading this next extract, think about what you already know about Maria's mother. Here she is, as a young woman. Compare what she becomes to how she begins.

***

My thirtieth birthday. It was like a movie moment, one of the few. A sunny day, breakfast in bed, then the girls and Charles coming through the door with my present. It was a big, rectangular box and it was wrapped in flowery paper with ribbons, ribbons with proper curls hanging down. I was so excited. I don't think I'd felt this excited for years. Even with the girls there, it was enough like the movies to make me happy.

'Open it, open it!' Jessie chanted. Her voice was always too shrill for me, she's always excited, no matter what's going on. It takes nothing at all to make her happy.

Maria stands there, with that simple smile of hers, Charles' hand on her shoulder, as if she needs holding up. She's fine, he worries about nothing. He's setting her up to be an invalid, a simpleton in a corner, someone who expects everyone to fetch and carry for them. She'll get nowhere with that attitude.

She smiles at me, excited in her own way over the present. I smile back; nothing can slow me down today. It must be something really good!

Paper off, I rip it artistically, letting it fall on the bed. Ribbons lay to one side and I see Jessie gathering them up to keep. The top of the box fits over the bottom, just like a dress box. I lift it, slowly, carefully, savouring the moment.

No tissue paper. I stop, holding the top of the box, looking down, not comprehending. It's too colourful for a dress.

'Do you like it?' Jessie, excited as ever. I set the lid next to me and touch the colours in the box. It's fabric, but not a dress.

'It's handmade, with special cloth,' Charles says. I look up fast enough to see him share a smile with Maria, like they're sharing a secret.

'Special cloth?' I ask, trying to recapture the movie moment as I pull out the bedspread and look at it, hiding my disappointment.

'When you cleared out all the old clothes last year,' Charles, still smiling, shows me a familiar patch on the corner of the bedspread, 'I saved them. This is Jessie's party dress, from when she was three. Remember?'

I did remember, she had it in a box, smaller than this one. That was her own movie moment.

'This is Maria's winter coat,' he points somewhere else. I'm losing interest by now.

'Here's your day coat, Mummy,' Jessie pulls at the piece nearest me and I look down, recognising the sky blue.

My eyes look across the bedspread, not recognising all the patches, though I will in time, even without them harping on about it. I see Maria's fingers, flicking at a corner of it, nervously twitching as she looks at me. I can see she knows I'm not pleased. The others are too dense to notice. On an impulse, she comes round the side of the bed and flings her arms around my neck,

'Happy birthday, Mummy,' she whispers.

For a second, I want to hug her back and have the birthday wishes. It's nice, just then, to have someone hold me and want nothing from me. Then I see a flash of colour out of the corner of my eye and feel angry all over again. I push her away, trying not to cry. How could they ruin my birthday and not even notice? How dare they pretend to care? This present cost next to nothing, I bet his mother made it! He might as well have asked for charity!

'Get out,' I whisper, low, but not too low for them to hear. I get some satisfaction from the way Charles and Jessie look when I speak. Maria, damn her, she turns her face away and doesn't look surprised. How dare she know me?

'Bonnie-' Charles reaches out his hand and I slap it away. He needn't come near *me* again.

I shake my head and flash my eyes at them. I know I must look beautiful as well as angry, I know how my eyes flash a deeper blue when I lose my temper. I know how well I look in my dark salmon night dress. I know Charles must want me, even with the girls here. I know how he thinks.

'Get out,' I say, more loudly, but not shouting yet. 'Leave me alone!'

With a twist and a kick, I throw the bedspread onto the floor and fling the top of the box after it. Jessie backs away, feeling for her father's hand.

'Mummy?' she asks, uncertain.

'Come on, love,' Charles guides her out.

Maria is the last to leave. She gives me a look I can't read. What is it? Sadness? Disappointment? As the door closes, I realise it was pity.

Then, that second, I begin to hate her. A little tramp, her father's daughter, giving me her pity! Well, she can have it back and then see how she likes it.

The colours, spilled out on the floor, taunt me. I almost fall out of bed in my haste, gather it up and, breaking my nail, push it through the open window. I watch as it tumbles into the back garden, landing on Maria's bicycle. The bicycle falls over and I hear the bell give a little *tring*.

Satisfied, I go back to bed. I know it won't be long before I'm crying over my sorry life, but for now, I'm content.

***

1. Explain how the events in this extract link to Maria's story.

This is the start of it all and should link with what we know of Maria's fate and the way her mother treated her.

2. Can we feel any sympathy for Bonnie?

You can decide yes or no for this question, but do try to show both sides. For instance, you may decide that Bonnie deserves no sympathy, while still explaining how *she* thinks she does. She feels very under-appreciated in this extract, even if she is mistaken.

3. How is Bonnie's personality portrayed in this extract?

Use evidence from the text, not forgetting that she is not yet the mother we met at the start of the book. Here she is still young and selfish. We don't know how she treats her family and her husband is there to protect the girls.

4. Describe the relationships Bonnie has with her daughters and husband in this extract.

Use quotes from the text and include any implied information, such as Bonnie criticising Jessie's high-pitched voice, which suggests she is probably often impatient with her.

5. "For now, I'm content." Explain what this quote tells us

about Bonnie.

Think of how she reacts to the 'bad' present and the satisfaction she gains from shocking them. Why is she now content? What has she done to make herself feel better? And why does having done this help her mood?

Twelve

Now we meet James, the grandson of Jessie and Edgar, the great-nephew of Maria. His section of the book is more traditional, told in the right order, from when he first goes into the house to the end of their story.

***

I never want to see another paintbrush. I come home from school and at first it's yay, we've got a new house, then ok, it's the haunted one and then I get a verbal slapping for calling it haunted in front of Grandma. And then I have to be all enthusiastic about making it like a real house that you can live in. We're 'making our mark'. Pity the other people didn't make more of their mark before they gave it up.

At least it's not really haunted. Mum thinks it is, but she hasn't said anything. I can see her looking when she comes in. I don't think she wants to live here really. She did before, she's talked about it with Dad. I've been eavesdropping so I know. But now it's nearly ready, she doesn't want to.

I think they should have done that room first though. I had nightmares about it, the night before we came for the first time. I dreamt I was in the fire and she was there. I could even see her, it was horrible. I had to put that right out of my mind or I couldn't ever live here. So, that's why I keep going in. I think of it like when you have to do something you don't like, or something scary, like reading out at assembly. The more you do it, the better it is. So every time I come, I have a look in the room, and every time I do that, it's a little bit better.

Still, I'm glad I don't believe in ghosts. Not proper ones. I will admit, there's an atmosphere. I was telling my friend Arran about it the other day. He wanted to know, again, if I'd seen the ghost. I told him there is no ghost, but there's something. He wanted to know what 'something' was. So I said, it's like an atmosphere but more. So then he wants to know what *that* is. In the end, I said it was like a bit of the past was stuck in the house and we were helping it to get out. He looked at me funny then. I think I looked at myself a bit funny too.

See, it wasn't until I said it that I realised that's what I've been doing when I go in the room. I feel like every time I go in, I'm letting a bit of the bad stuff out, making the house feel better. The rest of the house feels ok really, but that room won't, not til it's been sorted properly. Maybe one of these days I'll go in and it'll be just a room.

***

1. How does this extract link with Maria's story?

Explain about her room, what we know of her life, how she eventually escapes her room and sees the house in its modern state.

2. What kind of person is James?

How is his personality shown in this extract? Use evidence from the text.

3. How does James really feel about the house?

Using quotes, describe how he feels, as well as how he covers up his true feelings. Is he really fine about moving in? Is he afraid?

Thirteen

This extract describes how everything is going wrong for James, as he takes his final exams.

**

Who needs exams anyway? Who needs coursework, results, teacher's sarky comments and seeing everybody else writing when you're sitting there like your hands have fallen off? It doesn't matter, none of it matters. It's all a big con to get you to do what they want, when they want it. School. exams, uni, exams, job, job, job, which is like one exam after another, except you get paid.

I wouldn't have minded going away to uni, not really. That part sounded all right. It's the bit in the middle I can't do, the exams and then sixth form. When did that all have to happen? It's non-stop and I just want to slope off where nobody can find me and do my own thing.

All that revising and I didn't know half of what they were talking about. I used to know all the answers before, it's down the drain now. I don't know what happened.

It's like, well, imagine you have a big, shiny picture, with loads of colour on it. Doesn't matter what's on it, whatever you like. Let's say it's the harbour, full of boats and it's a sunny day. There's people walking past with dogs and little houses next to the water. It's all perfect looking. So, it's painted onto this enormous shiny paper, right? And you can look at the whole thing at once, or you can take your time and look at little bits of it, then take it all in. You have a choice.

Then, just when you're coming to have a look and thinking you know what's on the picture, somebody lets the sun in and it shines onto the picture. It bounces off the shiny paper, so if you look at it from the wrong angle, you can't see it, you're blinded. So you move round, to look from another angle, but you can only see some of it because it's in shade. Then you try again, and it's a blur of light and colours and nothing makes sense.

You have an idea of what it looked like before, when you could study it, but now you're all confused because it looks different, so different that you even doubt what you remember from before.

That's what it's like for me now. I was getting on fine, doing my own thing, revising and knowing it and then, Bam! It's like I can't see it properly anymore, and because I can't see it properly, I can't remember it properly either.

***

1. Re-write this extract in your own words, describing what has happened and how James feels about it.

This isn't as hard as it sounds. Make some notes about what is happening in each little section of the extract, then put them into proper sentences. A large part of the extract describes how James can no longer concentrate or remember things - find your own way to describe this confusion.

2. Compare James' description of his own confusion with the way Maria describes her confused state in the extract in Chapter Seven.

How do they both feel? How do they describe their feelings? What kind of language is used? Does James have more understanding of his emotions or is he just better at expressing himself?

Fourteen

James has gone to Maria's old house alone, to get away from worrying about exams. He is sitting in the back garden. As he falls asleep, he notices an old bike, a bag and a doll, lying in the back garden. When he wakes up, they have all gone.

***

Where's the bike gone? I realise I've been looking for it without knowing what I'm doing. Standing here, in the kitchen, I'm right behind where I was sitting outside. There's no bike at the edge of the garden now. Did someone come in?

I go out and look for it. No sign, and the bag's gone too. I walk to where it was, to see if any tracks lead away. When I get there, I'm not sure it's the right place. The path is completely overgrown.

I swish round, looking at the flower borders where the doll was lying. No borders, you'd never have known they were there except the grass is less thick under the trees. I go over to make sure, bend down, reach in, push around. Nothing.

No bike, no bag, no doll.

I lean, one hand on my knees, one hand in the grass where the borders used to be. My fingers reach back, trailing through the grass, and snag on something. It's amazing how cold a hot day can turn.

Like a madman (I am now a madman), I start pulling at the grass, my head bent under the edge of the trees, my knees getting green as I struggle to open up where I felt whatever it was.

Soil, more soil, clumps of grass sitting next to me, fingers full of grime and the smallest, little plastic foot sticking up into the sun. I swallow, suddenly feeling sick. I wish I was in the kitchen, drinking more water from the mini fridge.

Shaking my head, I carry on. Might as well be as mad as I can be and get it over with. Digging with your fingers is really hard, especially in summer with dry ground and nasty little stones in the soil. I have bleeding fingers by the end of it and I can hear my breathing, loud, like it belongs to somebody else.

Like I'm claiming a prize for God knows what, I drag out the doll and hold it above me, letting the sun shine on it. Yes, mad as I am, there's no denying it's the same doll. The blonde hair is muddy, the dress is ragged and rotten, the rest of it looks dirty but the same. A plain old doll, shaped like a little girl, not a creepy baby doll. Let's face I, all dolls are creepy, so this is still not good. But it's just a normal doll, that somebody buried.

Okay, *that* is creepy, even worse than me knowing where it was and seeing things that aren't there. Yes, well, I'll decide later which is creepier, because I think seeing things that aren't there is really scary, but we'll leave that for now. Seeing things is something that can happen to you, if your brain is melting or whatever. A person who buries dolls is worse than that.

I stand up, grunting as I realise my knees have locked with being so tense while I was digging it up. I actually stumble as I go into the kitchen. What must I look like now? Staggering about, covered in mud, holding a doll by the foot? A doll I just dug up?

I stand, washing off the mud and not stopping until the thing is clean. My hands are still dirty, I'll sort them later. I stand, holding her, looking back at the glass eyes staring up at me. I stroke her hair back from her face, so she looks more like she used to.

There's a few seconds there, when it's all quiet again and I almost forget where I am. I'm not freaked out by the doll anymore, though I try to pretend I am. If I'm freaked out, I'm admitting something abnormal happened. And it did. It just doesn't feel wrong, though. It feels right to have this doll here, all cleaned up and not in the ground anymore.

There's the cold chill again as it occurs to me - perhaps it was her doll? Or Grandma's?

What on earth am I supposed to do with it now? Go home and say, Grandma, you know that house you hated and we bought and now you have to go in all the time? Well, I found this doll, buried in the garden. Would you like it back?

I stare at the doll again, sitting upright on the work surface. I wash my hands without thinking about it, deciding what to do.

Sometime, some long ago time, that doll was bought as a present for a little girl. I don't know which little girl. One of them didn't make it, the other one is at my house, sticking up for me and trying to tell Mum that I've plenty of time to do what I need to, that there's more to life than exams.

My Grandma as a little girl, she hated this place, and

Grandma as she is now isn't keen either. But maybe she had this when she was happy? It might help. I should give her it.

***

1. "Seeing things is something that can happen to you, if your brain is melting or whatever. A person who buries dolls is worse than that." Explain what James means by this statement.

Think about how he feels about himself at the moment. He is suddenly unable to remember his revision work and is probably going to fail his exams. Now he has discovered a child's doll, buried in the garden of a house with a sad history.

2. What kind of language is used to describe James' feelings as he tries to find the doll, then digs it up? What impression does this give?

James is quite frenzied by the time he digs up the doll and does recognise he is not behaving very logically. Yet, he does find what he is looking for, so the situation is not logical.

Look at how the language shows his mood, as he frantically searches. Is he thinking rationally? Is he afraid? Is it clear how he feels or is this a moment where he is doing something without knowing why?

3. How do you view James' relationship with Jessie?

Look for the implied relationship, as much as for quotes which state she is willing to stand up or him or where he shows he cares about her. For instance, his decision to take the doll back to show her is complicated by him worrying he will upset her.

Fifteen

James has decided to give Jessie the doll, without explaining how he found it.

***

I kneel on the floor in front of her and bring the doll round, from behind my back. For a second she looks confused, not knowing what it is. Then her face changes and she goes very still. That seems to last a long time but I know it's not long because I can see my hand shaking, as I hold the doll, and it doesn't shake for long before she reaches out.

'Here, let me have it,' she speaks quietly, evenly. She's not shaking like I am, she's still calm and still. She holds the doll in front of her and looks at it, very closely. You can see she's checking it out, seeing if it's the right one. Her eyes scan over the hair, the face, the dress. You can't see much of the dress now it's rotted, but she seems to see enough.

Suddenly, her eyes are on me and I see the side of her that you usually don't see, past the smiles and the hugs and making everything all right. She looks me straight in the eye, dead centre, with me kneeling and her sitting, the doll between us.

'Where did you find it?' she whispers, her hand clutching it more tightly.

'In the garden,' I say. I really quickly flash through what I should tell her. Super quick, so there's only a second that I'm not talking. 'The foot was sticking out of the ground, so I dug it up.'

Okay, so I missed out the fact I had to pull out half the grass to find the soil but she doesn't ask. She looks at it, her face softer, her eyes travelling over it again, this time taking it in more slowly.

'She gave it to me, when I was older,' she smiles, not looking away from the doll. She spares a glance round the room, as if she's reminding herself where she is. 'When I was twelve,' she pauses, shaking her head. 'It was taken from me, I was too old for dolls.'

She twines a finger in the blonde hair. 'She's damp, did you wash her?'

I nod, gulping. It's like I expect her to know what happened, how I found the doll. Like I think she can see inside my head and know I'm not telling her everything.

She smiles again, to herself maybe? I don't know. She's looking at the doll and I know the smile isn't for me. Then she sits back and breathes in, deep and strong. Again, she looks right at me and I feel myself blushing. I can see her wondering why I'm blushing but, good old Grandma, she doesn't ask. Instead, she pushes herself forward on the sofa and kisses the top of my head.

'I can't often reach there anymore,' she says, laughing. I can see she isn't all the way through happy, but she doesn't seem upset. Relief!

I hug her, surprising us both. That doesn't happen often either, now I'm older. Sometimes, though, she's the best.

She stands up and looks at the doll in her hands. 'I'll leave her here,' she sets her on the sofa. 'She needs a new dress but that can wait. She's a toy and this is a playroom, so we'll leave her with the toys.'

'Don't you mind if Robert plays with her?'

She guides me out of the room, giving me a pat on the shoulder. 'She's a toy, James. I'm glad you found her, but she can stay in there and be what she is.' She looks up at me as she closes the door, her eyes crinkling in a proper smile.

**

1. How do you think Jessie feels in this extract? Give evidence for your answer, referring to past extracts.

Work through how Jessie reacts. She shows most of her emotions, though we can't be certain of what she is thinking. How does her reaction differ compared to how she might have reacted when she was younger? Think about how she is happy to let the doll be a toy and not a memory of Maria.

2. James and Jessie are very close. Do you agree or disagree?

Look at how they behave and what James thinks and feels about his grandmother. In what ways are they close? Is there any distance between them? For instance, he does not tell her how he found the doll.

3. Look at the extract in Chapter Nine and compare how Jessie is portrayed there and in this extract.

How is she different? In Chapter Nine, the extract is from her own point of view and you see how she tries to hide her feelings. In this extract, we see her through James' eyes. Is she the same person now? Do you think she is still hiding the way she feels, or is she happier and complete in the present day?

4. Write from Jessie's point of view and describe the moment when James gives her the doll.

This is your chance to look inside and see how Jessie really felt, when she held the doll again for the first time in so many years. Use evidence from the extract to help you and show how she moves from her initial shock to acceptance and happiness.

Sixteen

This extract is from near the very end of the book. As you read it, compare it with the extracts with Maria seeing the house as it is now and the scene when she sees Jessie again.

***

The sun comes in through the kitchen windows, the trees outside waving against the sky. For a time I can't measure, I feel the garden and the kitchen are the same place. I hear myself breathe in, breathe out, the moment stretching longer than it should, Robert and Granddad beside me but somewhere else.

Across the room, the sunbeams settle onto a shape. An instant when they silhouette a girl, turned towards us, her hand outstretched. Everything in me stops and I stare, unmoving, unbreathing, staring into the sun as it lands on the air around her.

She looks at me, her face unclear, her lips open, her hair around her shoulders almost showing a wisp of colour. I look back, the longest moment of all, when I see she is already fading.

The sun that touched her, the sunbeams which landed on her shoulders, they're left behind as the space is empty once more. The time it took was an instant, though longer for me, much longer than it should have been. I breathe out again, all is like it should be again.

I feel the warmth of the kitchen, the light through the window, see the trees waving in the breeze. The door is wide open and there is nothing but what we can see to be lit by the sun.

I look up at Granddad, the way he laughs with Robert. She reached out to him. I hope, wherever she is, someone reached back.

***

1. Looking at the language used, what is your impression of this moment?

Think about the type of descriptive words used, such as the warmth of the kitchen or the fact Maria was framed by sunlight. What overall impression does it give, to use this kind of imagery?

2. How does James feel at this moment?

Use evidence from the text and describe how you think he feels, as well as how he is portrayed in the extract.

3. What is the significance of James' only glimpse of Maria being in the kitchen?

Consider how often James has been in her old room, 'letting the atmosphere out'. If he believed the house was haunted, then he probably expected to see Maria in her old room. Why is it important that she was in the kitchen instead?

Seventeen

1. Without re-reading any of the extracts, do brief character biographies for Maria, Jessie, Edgar, Bonnie and James.

What is most memorable about each of them? What details can you remember? What kind of people were they? Don't worry if you forget some details, write about your impressions of each person.

2. Find a quote for each character, which sums up their personality for you. It must be a direct quote from one of the extracts.

This should really serve as a one-line reminder of who and what the character is, so choose carefully!

3. Re-read all of the extracts, then write your own summary of what has happened in 'the rain comes'.

This one will take some time. Do read the extracts again, even if you think you can remember everything. When you write your summary, try not to use too many details but be careful to include anything important.

4. Describe the house, as it was when Maria lived there.

Imagine you are walking through the rooms, unseen. You can include descriptions of the people too, but it should mainly be about the house.

5. Now describe the house as it is in the present day.

You don't need to compare it to your piece about the house in the past, but you can include details about the same things. Make it feel as if you are really there and can see everything.

6. Imagine you are James and write about what happens after you have moved into the house.

How much has changed? Are you happy there? Do the exams turn out all right?

Use what you know of his personality to write this and don't be afraid to make up new situations for him, that have nothing to do with the story you already know.

7. Edgar and Jessie are leaving on a holiday. Describe the scene as they say goodbye to James and his family.

You can do this from the viewpoint of either character, or from the outside looking in. You should explain how they feel, perhaps what memories come back to them. Do they feel like it's a normal holiday or does it seem significant that the family is back in the old house and now they can leave?

8. Finally, describe Maria's old room, twenty years from now, as Robert decorates it for someone to use.

Robert is James' little brother and will only be about twenty four for this exercise. He probably doesn't remember living anywhere else but this house and its sad past will not really have touched him.

Will there be any reminders of Maria's time or will your story be a happy interlude, as Robert decorates what is only a bedroom? And who is going to stay there?

Section 2: Original Writing & Language

This section is intended to brush up your writing and language skills. I have included questions which are similar to ones you might encounter in exams, as well as exercises which help you develop writing techniques and learn how to approach and solve literacy-based tasks.

Some of the work in here may be more complicated than you are used to, but by learning how to work through these exercises, you will find it easier when you have to do similar tasks in exams and coursework.

I have included guidelines and suggestions for all the activities in here, to give you a helping hand. If you have real difficulty with any of the exercises, leave it and move on to the next one. It's much better to do this than stress over one problem when you could be working more happily on another.

Creative Renovation

When you renovate a building, you take what is already there and repair it, replacing what you need to make it whole again. For the next two exercises, we're going to do the same with creative writing. I will give you the base for a story and you will create something new using that base.

Don't worry if this sounds daunting, or you have never done it before. Using a base for a story can be hard at first, but it also gives you the ideas for the story, meaning you can concentrate on building it up into a new 'shape'. Your own ideas will happen, once you become used to thinking about original writing in a different way.

You can also try this idea as many times as you like, with poems or stories you find for yourself. These are just to help you learn the technique but sometimes you need to find base material that interests you personally, before it really takes off for you.

The Knitting Witch

For this first exercise, you are going to use The Knitting Witch as the base for a story. This is a non-rhyming poem with a free structure.

The witch sits and knits,

Her patchwork world

Coming to life in her lap

Seas broil as she shifts to reach the thread

People scream when she sews them together,

Fixed forever in a square of her making

As she knits, it grows,

Becoming round and real

The squares curving to meet one another

She grins, hunched over her world, her work

When she is done, all dandy-ness and fine measure,

She pulls up the last stitch, seals it together

And hides the knot under an ice-floe

Her legs unfold beneath the world,

Its mountains soft against her knees.

She rubs her nose and nods,

Approving

The last piece of thread is slipped from the needle

And tucked in her pocket

One small shaft of sunlight kept

From the world at her feet

Look at the poem itself. Turning it into a story is easier than with some poems, as it doesn't have a rhyming structure that naturally makes it sound like a poem. If you were to rearrange the lines into proper sentences, it would still make sense.

If you are not used to dealing with poetry, firstly do just that - take the sentences out of the poem and rearrange them into normal sentences, with punctuation and spacing where necessary. You want to make it look like a couple of paragraphs describing the witch, rather than it being a poem anymore.

Once you have done that, read through it again and see how it changes the whole piece of writing just by rearranging the way it looks on the page.

(This is a handy hint for dealing with poems in general: if they make you nervous, try rearranging them into prose instead and see if they look less scary. This doesn't always work though - some poems are scary no matter what you do with them!)

Now, you need to turn The Knitting Witch into a proper story. By breaking it down from its poetic structure, it has become a series of sentences. To then make these into a proper story, you need to add detail, as well as adding more punctuation and extra ideas to plump it out into a nice, round story.

Think about what happens in the poem. The witch is knitting and as she knits, her creation comes to life and is a real world with people in it. Imagine the witch, a giantess to her world, as she knits and the word grows in her lap, with her hunched over it. No wonder the people scream!

What will you do with this imagery in your story? Will you follow the ideas as they are and make it into a horror story or fantasy? Or will you create something more mysterious, where no one can see the witch but the world is still coming to life? Or is it an ordinary world, like ours, with extraordinary things happening in it - caused by the witch, but unknown to the people?

You can do anything you like for this, as long as you use the information already there in the poem. Add as much as you like, but try not to take anything away. If you decide to make the witch unknown or invisible to her world, then try to hint at her existence by making things happen.

If this seems like a lot to do all at once, then try using the poem for the first set of sentences, then writing down more ideas as bullet points. Make it small and simple to begin with, then build from there into a fuller story.

Most of all, don't worry about how it turns out. All of this is just practice to help you and will not be marked. You can do it again, if you like, or try the same idea on a different poem to see how it works with other poems and ideas. If it seems really hard, then try using a very short poem that gives you a simple idea as a story base.

Sammy Saves the Day

This is a simple, short story aimed at small children. Each line or two would usually be on one page of a picture book, so that the story is as much about looking at the pictures as hearing or reading the words.

Read the story, then re-write it as a horror story, aimed at either older children, young adults or adults. You can add as many extras as you like and can also change some things within the original story. However, try not to change too much, as the aim is to build on what you've been given, rather than taking things away.

This should be easier than using the poem as a story base because this is already in the form of a story. A good way to start is by noting down anything extra you want to happen. For instance, do you want to include more drama when Sammy keeps climbing to high places at the start of the story? Does Mrs Harper really have her hand stuck in the plughole, or is there something trying to drag her through it? Is Sammy really a nice person, or will he turn out to be the villain of the piece?

The choice is yours. Keep it simple to start with, then build your story using Sammy Saves the Day as your foundations.

When Sammy grew up he wanted to be a firefighter and rescue people.

Every day he practiced running very fast and climbing things.

His mother was always finding him stuck in high places.

She told him if he wasn't careful he would be the one who needed to be rescued.

One day he heard a scream from next door. Someone was in trouble!

He rushed round, pushing on his helmet and grabbing his little ladder.

Old Mrs Harper had her hand stuck in the sink. Sammy knew just what to do.

He set his ladder next to her and climbed up next to the sink.

He poured oil down the plug until Mrs Harper's fingers were all slippy.

Then he helped to pull up her hand until, with a pop! she was free.

Mrs Harper was very happy to be rescued. She gave Sammy a full plate of chocolate cookies and told him he'd make a great firefighter when he grew up.

Sammy went home feeling very happy. Now he knew he could rescue people and he didn't even have to be grown up to do it.

But his mother said he still wasn't allowed on the roof.

The Dreaded Letter Writing

In real-life, we all send emails and, very occasionally, a letter. In schools, college and the world of exams, we all seem to write letters - have you noticed? So many tests and exams include a letter writing activity, usually to someone in authority.

For this exercise, we're also going to write letters. I want you to do this as practice for when letters crop up in exams and also as a way of developing your skills at writing for different occasions. You see, even if you never write another letter, you will be communicating with people by email, online form, messaging and so on and sometimes those communications will need to be as formal as a letter.

However, having said all that, you do get to have a bit of fun with this one.

Letter One: Write an anonymous letter to your headmaster. He never reads emails anyway and you don't want him to find out who it's from. Tell him exactly what you think of him and the way he runs the school. Describe the mess he made of reinventing sports day. Say what you think of his assemblies.

Suggest a new job for him. In other words, tell him everything you've been desperate to get off your chest since the first day you started at his school.

Make the letter quite formal, but not polite. No swearing, and no doodles that you couldn't show your granny. Keep it like a letter, while making sure he knows what you think.

Having written the letter and put it to one side to post, you almost forget about it until a few days later when your mother says,

'Oh, I meant to tell you. I saw that letter you forgot to post and I handed it in when I went to school the other day. I told the head I'd had it in my bag, in case he blamed you for sending it in late. I'm sure he'll be impressed that it was hand delivered!'

Your blood runs cold. The amount of trouble you are now in cannot be measured by any ruler made by man. It's not long before you are called into the headmaster's office and have to answer for your crime.

Letter Two: You either have to make it up to him or be expelled. How would you put it right? What could you say or do? Write him another letter, this time a much nicer one, offering to put things right.

As part of your groveling, say nice things about his assemblies, find good descriptions for what he did to Sports Day and say why he is perfect for the job of headmaster of your school.

In part, this second letter is a re-write of the first, but takes everything back you said before. You also need to add your heartfelt apology as well as offering to make it up to him. This letter is still formal but the language should all be focused on making your headmaster feel good about himself and more likely to forgive you.

These two letters are not the type of thing that would come up in exams. They are more difficult, with different elements to them. By managing more complicated exercises like this, the exam/test letters should not seem so hard in future. But do resist the urge to use some of your headmaster-teasing language from the letters you do at home!

Diary of a dog-walker

For this exercise, you are going to practice original writing with descriptive language.

You have volunteered at the local kennels and are writing a blog for the school website.

Describe each day that you go to the kennels. Include the dogs you meet and what happens to them. Encourage people to rehome or donate to the kennels

Have at least five entries for your diary/blog. You can keep the language chatty and informal, but do try to use different ways of describing how you feel and what you see. Also, change how you feel as time passes, to show your reactions to being at the kennels.

How would your entries change? Would you get more or less attached to the dogs? Would you lose interest or would it affect what you wanted to do with your life?

It can be a good idea to start by being less personal and more descriptive of the surroundings, such as describing the kennels, the dogs you see, the other people who work there.

Then, as time passes, you could become more involved yourself and would describe your feelings more often, or using emotive words like, 'poor old Barney' or 'sad little Rex', or 'the terrible sight of an empty kennel'.

Bear in mind that you are being informal and honest about the way you feel, but you are also writing a blog that anyone can see, including people you have to meet at school every day. How would this change what you included? Would you be more wary of what you wrote? Would you try to be aware of it at first, then be too carried away by the dogs' plight to worry?

You can also include spaces in your blog for pictures of the dogs. This would be essential if you wanted people to get involved or donate, so don't forget to add little sections where you might have a space (you don't need a real picture) along with a label saying, 'Freddie before he found his forever home'.

Join the club!

Leaflet: Write a leaflet to attract people to your new club. You want to make it sound really good, while using language that will appeal to the people who might be interested. Think about what kind of club to advertise - it doesn't have to be one you would join in real life.

For instance, if you decided on a new rock-climbing club, you might want to use words that suggest adventure, challenge, teamwork, learning new skills, extreme sports and so on.

Separate your leaflet into sections. You'll need headings, pictures, lots of colours, bold text, quotes and reviews. If you are unsure how these all apply to leaflets, get hold of some leaflets in real-life and see how they are laid out. Sometimes it seems like all the above are more important than the actual information!

Once you are happy you have enough information, design a mock-up of the leaflet. You don't need to use real pictures, but detail where they will be and what they are about. Don't forget the basics like contact details and times/dates the club will be on.

Interview: Write an interview with someone who has been to the club or taken their children and make a TV advert out of what they say. This isn't as scary as it sounds!

Write the interview as if you are asking someone questions about your club, then filling in their answers. This way you will build up quite a lot of information, such as how much they or their children enjoyed it, how often they have been (important, as this shows they are keen to keep attending), why they would recommend it to other people.

Advert: Once you have your interview, you can the script for a TV advert. This starts with the interview written down in a simple form, without your questions. So, rather than you asking the person if they would recommend the club and them answering, your script might look like this:

Person: I would really recommend people try the Jaunty Juniors club. My little boy Eric has been much easier to live with since he started going. He's even too tired to bother the cat!

You also need to include what will happen on screen, as you don't want the whole advert to just be the person talking to camera. So, while they are recommending the club, you could have a shot of little Eric running around the Jaunty Juniors club, bouncing off the other children and leaping into the ball pool.

Your script directions for this might look like:

Cut to Eric, running from door to ball pool. Cut back to parent.

Writing the script for your TV advert might seem difficult at first, but keep in mind how most adverts are very short and show strong ideas in attention-seeking ways. If you are making an advert for your club, it doesn't have to be a very expensive looking one, like you would see on primetime TV. It can be a simple one, meant for local TV, aimed specifically at people who live near you. Your budget would be different, meaning you can keep it quite basic.

If in doubt, look at some adverts on TV, local and national, and imagine how you would write down the script for them. How many directions would you have compared to talking? How would you describe what you see on screen?

Storyboards: If you like, you can include even more detail by creating storyboards, which show all the main events of your advert in pictures. This one is optional, but can be a really good way to see how words become actions on screen.

Then and now

Here is an extract from a magazine for young women and girls, published more than 100 years ago, in 1912. Read it through, taking notice of what it is talking about and the language used.

The little things that count

When a people get lax in the little things, it is not a long step to laxity in the big things. And we are getting to be criminally lax in the smaller things. One hears on every side the complaint of the failure of the small courtesies. Notes are left unacknowledged; engagements are not kept, nor the reasons explained; courtesies extended receive no recognition. It has even got the point where presents fail of proper and just thanks. Too much is being taken for granted. Money has become too plentiful, our pace is so fast; relative values are all getting muddled up, and the little courtesies that sweeten life are either lost sight of or lack proper and courteous recognition. It is not that we do not know our manners. We do. But our lives are too rushed, and rush always means carelessness.

We cannot afford to make our lives so busy as to render ourselves insensible to the little thought that comes to us from another; from the seemingly small courtesy; from the apparently insignificant present. With these and in these are sometimes found the deepest thoughts, the truest friendship, and the only true thing that, after all is said and done, is worth holding on to in life. The little thing is here the big thing.

1. Write a summary of the main points in this extract.

Some of it may be harder to understand, but the general purpose is probably clear. Don't worry too much about the details at this stage.

2. Give examples of language that is used in a different way from how we might use it today.

This happens throughout this extract. The way words are arranged, the types of words used (like laxity) are understandable as the English language, but are unusual in modern usage.

3. Give examples of the way punctuation is used differently from today.

This is slightly harder, but look at the length of sentences, use of semi-colons and commas. What would we do with them today? Would they be in the same places?

4. Pretend the article was written today. Do you agree with the writer of this article?

You will have heard plenty of people complain about the lack of manners. I think there is something reassuring in seeing the same complaint in such an old magazine. Perhaps all is not yet lost!

Write a few paragraphs about whether or not you agree with the general themes of the article. Explain your opinion and quote the article in your work, to show you have understood it.

5. Re-write the article into modern language.

Yes, the whole thing! What should you change or rearrange? How can you word it so that you lose none of the meaning but it becomes a modern piece? What do you need to add or take out?

If you find some of it difficult to understand, use a dictionary or discuss it with someone else. Sometimes, simply reading it out loud makes the meaning more clear as the words sound more familiar spoken than written down.

Story Starters

For this exercise, you need to write a story based on the story starters given below. You don't need to do all of them but could come back and try other exercises later. This kind of question is often given in exams, so it's always useful to practice writing a story with very little guidance.

1. Think of a time when you have hurt someone's feelings.

Yes, this kind of thing is a favourite of exams and tests everywhere. Really, I do hope you make up your answer as they have no business wanting to know such personal information!

(Only kidding, it can be really useful to write about your own experiences because you know all the facts. But there is no harm in making it up as sometimes life isn't as exciting as fiction).

What they are mainly looking for is a good descriptive type of story, where you can explain what happened and keep it clear and interesting. Don't go off into tirades of feeling but do include how you felt and why.

If you are writing in the first person, do remember to also describe how other people behave and seem to feel as it makes the story more interesting for the reader.

2. "Don't come near me!" he screamed. Write a story with this as your first sentence.

This is a classic kind of story starter, were they give you the start or the end of the story.

Take my advice: if given the choice, choose the one that starts the story as you may not have time to finish the one with the ending or may go astray in the middle of writing it and not know how to connect your story to the end line.

Having said all of that, here is an ending line to try out.

3. And then we were friends again. Write a story with this as the last line.

See number 2 for guidance.

4. There were bunnies everywhere. Write a funny story based on this line.

It's trickier to write a story that has a definite theme, but it can be a really good choice if you are comfortable with the subject. However, trying to write something funny in the middle of an exam is perhaps not the best combination. It's amazing how un-funny exams can be.

5. The ship dipped past the last wave and came into sight.

A nice, general story idea which might or might not spark your imagination. This could be a gift if you have an idea to go with it and is usually manageable even if you don't feel very kindly towards it.

The good thing about more general writing prompts is that you have more freedom to write what you like. This is also why you should be careful. Always remember to make things interesting, descriptive and relevant to the question. Also, keep an eye on the clock so that you have enough time left to finish your story and check it over afterwards.

6. "No! I won't do it!" Write a story about an argument.

This is similar to other story ideas, but you need to include a lot more dialogue. Sometimes it makes a good story to have lots of dialogue, compared to describing more and having less talking. Be aware that you should still include details and keep the story moving, even if it is mostly talking.

Page | 104

7. I couldn't believe my eyes.

This is a 'write anything' story prompt as just about any situation could end with your character feeling disbelief. This is a good kind of story to try if you like to use your own ideas but perhaps not so good if you need more guidance.

8. Write about your first day somewhere.

This is another favourite in tests, whether it's writing about your first day at school or when you moved house to live somewhere new. The story should have a good mix of description – your first impressions of a place and people – as well as explaining how you were feeling and what you thought about it all.

In the movies

This exercise is a longer one, with stages to work through. Don't feel you have to do it all at once. I have included lots of example answers to help you.

You are going to write about a TV show where kids aged 12-15 compete for the chance to make their own movie. The contestants have to go through different stages to prove their idea is the best. The winner will be chosen by votes from school children across the UK.

Think of two characters. These will be your contestants in the show. Write down their names, ages, girl/boy and **two other facts** about them. Think about how they can be different from one another as this will make it easier to write about them separately.

My contestant is Jen: *Jen is a 14 year old girl and is very small for her age. When she grows up she wants to be a vet.*

Each of the following exercises must be done **twice**, once for each of your contestants. Keep in mind a very clear idea of what type of person they are and how they will present their ideas and themselves.

Genre

The children have to decide which genre their movie will be. Will their choice be influenced by what you have already said about them or their ages? For instance, if you have a younger contestant, they might want an adventure film whereas an older one might like sci-fi or horror.

Choose from below or create new ones.

Horror, comedy, romance, adventure, musical, thriller, murder mystery, sci-fi, fantasy

Write a very short, simple description of your contestants' movie ideas.

This can be as short as a couple of sentences, depending on how easy it is to explain. You want the kind of short description that would tell someone in a few words, what the movie would be about.

For example, Jen might say:

My movie is an adventure about a girl who finds a dolphin on the beach and it becomes her friend.

You see how you have the whole movie in only a few words?

Write a detailed description of your movie idea, including who it will appeal to and why you want to do it.

This is where you need to include more information, being careful not to ramble on. For this one, Jen might say:

Suzi finds a dolphin on the beach near her new home. She calls it Crystal and they become best friends. Then the evil fisherman tries to catch Crystal and Suzi must stop him before it's too late.

This movie will appeal to children who like animals and adventure. I want to do it because I love dolphins and think everyone needs to understand them more.

Do you see how Jen's description builds on the shorter one, giving you more idea of the film's plot? It also shows you it's going to include some drama as well as the friendship of girl and dolphin.

Jen's reason for doing the film is important. She wants people to understand dolphins more, so she isn't just wanting to film a cosy animal story. As your contestants are competing on a game show, presented to the public, it's a good idea to include good reasons why their films should be chosen.

The Plot

You need to create a simple plot for your contestants' movies, either in bullet points or short paragraphs. Describe what will happen, who your main characters are and, if you know it, the end of the movie.

Don't stress about making this perfect. You can change things later on. By now you should have a fair idea of what your films are about, so writing down the main plotline can be seen as an extension of what you have already decided.

Here is Jen's plotline:

Suzi moves to the new house and explores the beach. She meets Crystal for the first time. They become friends. Suzi sees Crystal every day.

The fishing boat appears. An evil fisherman shouts at Crystal and throws rocks at her. He threatens Suzi. Suzi is told to stay away from the beach.

She creeps back to check on Crystal and the dolphin is nowhere to be seen. Suzi must find Crystal before it is too late.

Suzi tracks down the fisherman. He has captured Crystal and trapped her in a glass case. He is going to sell her. He is not really a fisherman, he is a criminal.

He chases Suzi and almost captures her when Crystal bursts out of the glass case and distracts him. He slips on the broken glass and as he falls, Crystal butts him with her head. He is knocked out.

Suzi calls the police and Crystal is saved. The criminal is put in prison. Crystal and Suzi are friends forever.

A scene

Now write a short scene from the movie. There must be some dialogue, but you can decide if there will be lots of talking or only a few words. Don't forget to describe any direction for your actors, such as *'Suzi goes towards the field and screams'*.

Here is Jen's scene:

Suzi sneaks out of the house, carrying her bag. At the beach we hear Crystal calling for her.

Crystal appears in the water. Suzi paddles to the big rock.

Suzi: I have the pictures to show you, of my friends from back home.

Suzi looks sad.

Suzi: My old home anyway. Here, look.

Suzi holds each picture up and Crystal nods and chatters back to her.

Camera pans away to show Suzi and Crystal together, the sun behind them. Fishing boat appears in the distance, getting closer. They don't notice.

Characters

You need to decide what your films' characters look like and what kind of people they are. This shouldn't be too difficult now you have done your plotlines and example scenes. You should have a clearer idea of who will need to be in your contestants' films.

Think of two or three main characters and write mini-biographies for them. Also create at least one supporting character.

Explain how they all know each other or how their relationships develop through the movie.

Here are Jen's characters:

Suzi is 14 years old and very lonely. She has one brother who is much older. She lives with her mother and brother at their new house by the sea and wishes she could move back to their old home.

Crystal is a wild dolphin who becomes best friends with Suzi. She is kind and intelligent and brave. She seems to understand what Suzi says and talks back to her.

The evil fisherman turns out to be a criminal who is on the run from the police. He will do anything for money and doesn't care who he hurts.

My supporting character is Suzi's mum who wants her daughter to be happy and wishes she could make new friends. She is very busy and goes out to work a lot.

Can you think of any famous actors who might play your characters? This can help you to imagine them more clearly.

Action Scene

Write a very descriptive action scene for your movie, with or without dialogue. Try writing it as a story first, then changing it into script direction, as this makes it easier to write without thinking about how to set it out or change it for direction.

Here is Jen's action scene:

Suzi hears Crystal calling, but can't get to her. The warehouse is dark and creepy and she runs through spider webs and bangs into big boxes.

Suzi comes round a corner and knocks over a crate. The evil fisherman looks up and sees her. Suzi sees Crystal, trapped in a glass case next to a truck.

The fisherman gives chase, one hand clenched in a fist, the other holding a hammer. Suzi runs but can't find the way out. The fisherman corners her and reaches for her.

A smashing sound makes him turn and Crystal calls and calls. Suzi darts past the fisherman and runs to the dolphin.

The evil fisherman follows, slipping on the wet ground and shards of glass which are all that's left of the glass crate.

He bends, falling and Crystal head butts him. He crashes to the ground, unconscious.

The Twist

Either at the end of the movie or during it, there should be a surprise twist.

This one should be something extra to the information you have already given in your plotline and scenes. Where could you insert a twist? What is it and who does it affect? Will you keep it a secret before the film is released?

Here is Jen's twist:

Suzi's brother discovers the evil fisherman used to own the little house they are renting. He finds some loose floorboards in his room and finds an old safe hidden away in there. It is the jewellery the fisherman hid from his last criminal job.

Suzi and her family return the jewellery to the old lady who owned it and are given a big reward. They also become good friends with the old lady.

Where?

Where do you think most of your filming should be done, when not in the studio? Which country or type of location would suit it best? Do you need desert or beach? Mountain or rubbish dump?

Describe your location/s, explaining why they are important to the movie.

Here is Jen's location:

I would like my film to be made in Scotland because we had a holiday home there and it was really beautiful, all wild and windy with lots of exciting and secret beaches.

It would suit the film to be filmed in lots of different weather, showing how long Suzi and Crystal are friends and there is always lots of weather in Scotland.

Why me?

This is where the contestants must sell themselves. Write a speech for them to say to the audience, explaining why they and their movie idea would be the best and what it would mean to them to win.

If you like, you can make this speech intentionally bad, which would either mean your contestant loses or people feel sorry for them and vote anyway.

Here is Jen's speech:

I think you should choose my film as there are lots of films already made about nasty things happening to people and not enough about the friendships we can have with animals. It's really important for people to understand the natural world, so that even if you're not an animal lover, you can appreciate why you shouldn't harm them and why we should all look after the planet.

When I grow up I want to be a vet and I want to help other children and adults as well to see animals as a vital part of all our lives, even if we live in towns and cities and only ever see pets. I think making good films about animals can help people to appreciate them and may also make other children grow up wanting to work with animals.

Please choose me as I'm very passionate about my film and I have good reasons for wanting to make it. Even if I'm not chosen, I'll try and get the film made as I care about it so much.

Almost there

Your two contestants have made it to the final and are against each other. After all this effort, their films are on the brink of being made.

As part of the final, they each have a scene from their scripts filmed, acted out by children from their school. Write an article for a school magazine, describing what happens on set and how the filmed scenes turn out in the end.

This article can be from your own point of view, as someone from the school, so you can now describe your contestants from a more objective viewpoint.

Here is the article for Jen's school:

We all love our Jen, don't we? Which is why our kids tried their hardest to make her scene a success. We all remembered the time she brought the ferrets into school and they got off and took three days to be captured. Jen makes everything more exciting and we know she'll do a great job with this film.

Unfortunately, our acting could have been better. There's been a terrible cold going round school and the only one who didn't suffer from it was Miss Wilkinson who kept having to scream her head off before anyone could hear her - their ears are blocked up as well as their noses.

Owen was brilliant as Crystal the dolphin. I never knew he could make a noise like that. It took a bit of practice, but he was soon squealing and rattling like a proper marine mammal. I think he got a bit carried away when Freddie turned up, as the evil fisherman. We ended up having to re-shoot that part because dolphins aren't meant to fight with their fists.

All in all we did Jen proud and I can't wait to see if she's won. She's promised us all a tour of the film studio if she gets through.

The winner!

After all this, one of your contestants has won!

Decide which contestant is the lucky winner. They are going to write a blog entry, describing what happened when they won, how they felt, what has happened since and if anything unexpected has surfaced since the end of the competition.

Don't be afraid to include quite a lot of detail or to let a good amount of time pass before the writing of the blog entry. This could be something written as their finished film is about to be released, many months later, or it could be written the day after the competition. What differences would this bring to the blog?

Here is Jen's blog:

At last, my dream is coming true! It seems like a dream still, when I walk onto set and there is Mr G, my brilliant evil fisherman. He couldn't be better! And so evil, I can't tell you! Except only on screen, off screen he's lovely.

Benito the dolphin is brilliant too. They tell me no one will know he's a boy, though I'm not sure about that. I did try to persuade them to use a girl but they don't listen to everything you say. That was one of the surprises when it all happened, how much they don't listen. But then, seeing it all being filmed and making friends like Mr G make it all worthwhile.

The girl who plays Suzi is a brand new actress. I wish we could be friends, I really do. She is perfect, honestly, the perfect Suzi. It's like they took her out of my brain and put her on screen. Off screen? Well, the first day she actually kicked Benito!!! I couldn't believe it! Mr G took her to one side and talked to her. I don't know what he said, but she's been a lot better since then.

In a few days, I'll get to see the finished film. I'm almost crying as I write this. I kind of don't want it to end, even though it's all been for this moment. It's been such a massive thing in my life and now I have to leave it all behind and start my exams.

Really, I'm not leaving it behind because I've changed my mind about becoming a vet. I was talking about it with Mr G and he knows some people who do wildlife documentaries and that's what I'm going to do. I'll be able to carry on spreading the word about how important animals are and our natural world and I'll reach loads more people than being a vet.

I can't wait!

Printed in Great Britain
by Amazon